NET GENERATORS
OF
MISERY

(abridged)

ISBN: 9781659794519

published: June, 2020

author: *M.S.*

netgen0mis@gmail.com

Sometimes people use "respect" to mean "treating someone like a person" and sometimes they use "respect" to mean "treating someone like an authority"

and sometimes people who are used to being treated like an authority say "if you won't respect me I won't respect you" and they mean "if you won't treat me like an authority I won't treat you like a person"

and they think they're being fair but they aren't, and it's not okay.

- someone on reddit

special thanks to:
the intellectual dishonesty, lack of discernment
& casual disregard on the parts of
Officers ▓▓▓▓ & Crowe of Seaside, OR.

This book would not have happened
without you.

Also, an acquaintance would like to know,
what chop-shop is the department sending
"abandoned" BMW's to these days?

This book is dedicated to:

Leonard Peltier.
Occupy Wall Street protesters.
Civil Rights marchers.
everyone wrongfully evicted from their home.
those who protested US involvement in Viet Nam.
Native Americans.
Black America.
the Latino community.
marijuana users continuing to serve time
in states that have legalized.

This book is dedicated to:
sex workers & raped arrestees.
kids in the school-to-prison pipeline.
the memory of those who fought for women's right to vote.
the homeless.
ex-cons trying to move forward with honor.
those who fought for unions,
40 hour work weeks
and living wages.
those harassed for feeding the homeless.
people of conscience.

This book is dedicated to:
gay human beings.
those who stood at & with NoDAPL.
Water Is Life.
the families of civilians killed in no-knock raids.
the wrongfully imprisoned.
the Boystown ~~kids~~ adults still recovering.
owners of any animal that might make a "peace" officer feel threatened.

This book is dedicated to:
the anonymous George Floyds
a camera never recorded,
whose deaths went unwitnessed & unexploited,
if not unmourned.

This book is dedicated to all those for whom
"law enforcement" & "peace" officers
made bad situations
unjustifiably worse.

I was arrested for something I didn't do. Though my charges were dismissed and the overall consequences far, far less than they could have been, my life was upended, destabilized, huge opportunities lost and personal resources wasted because "law enforcement" in the United States simply does not prioritize accuracy or honesty.

As of this writing, I am still under increased legal strictures, at major risk of identity theft and stolen items remain unreturned primarily due to the motivated reasoning and questionable discernment of "law enforcement".

This is hardly the first time I've experienced directly, or watched first hand, "peace" officers' deliberate intellectual dishonesty and casual disregard for the consequences of their actions on others.

Though none of my experiences remotely compare to the horrors so many honest, law abiding U.S. Citizens have gone through at the hands of "peace" officers, my personal experiences only reinforce what both local and national news in the U.S. so often show: the institution of "law enforcement" in the U.S. is not worthy of it's power.
Nor strives to be.

Liars, leeches, murderers, thugs and thieves. It seems the cops that aren't failing their communities are covering for the ones who are.

More importantly, our courts, legal system and elected officials are letting the shit slide. In the United States of America, "peace" officers shot dead almost 1000 people in 2015 and every one was ruled justified. Yeah. OK. Similar examples of leeway are countless.

It does not take much objective study to realize "law enforcement" as practiced in the United States was always intended to be corrupt or corruptible. Such corruption will seek out and nurture a psychology all too willing to believe one can trade moral agency for power.

Evil flourishes when good people stand aside.

Our nation's "law enforcement" too often becomes
an evil that good people should
no longer stand aside for.

BE a citizen. See something? Say something. **Do** something.
Freedom isn't free and must be defended from all enemies,
foreign & domestic.
- M.S.

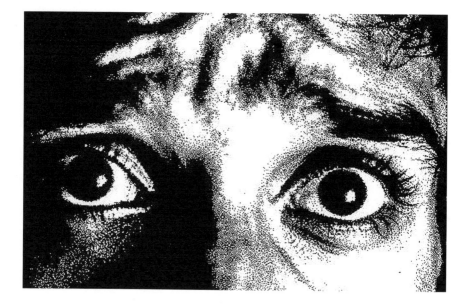

Violence. Threats. Fear. Coercion.

What honest craftsman
with a desire to build anything positive
uses those tools almost exclusively?

What can be built
by the trade relying on those tools
but mounds and barriers
bulldozed from the rubble
of other people's lives?

Obstacles
the rest of us
have to navigate?

To seek a career in

"law enforcement"

 is to seek

a profession

where the primary skill set

is being willing to

 intimidate,

harass,

cite,

detain,

and

kill

one's own

fellow citizens,

regardless of outcome.

Is the law

viewed

by "law enforcement"

as something

that should be

a stable platform

for everyone

to build

a life

on?

Or

is the law

simply a means

for "peace" officers

to accumulate

and wield

power?

More and more people,

average people,

non-criminals,

non-societal dregs,

positive contributors,

are believing

less of the former

and more

of the latter.

Are cops
net generators
of
misery?

Should just seeking a job in

"law enforcement"

raise red flags

among friends & family?

Does the judgmental a-hole
sticking their nose
in everyone else's business
make a workplace
or job-site
more efficient or pleasant?

At what point
do hall monitors
start retarding
freedom,
innovation,
and driving
good people to
just quit?

At what point
does "law enforcement"
become an undue burden
on communities
and simply become
sand in the gears?
If not a legit threat to
Life & Liberty for All?

Shouldn't remaining in

a profession

accepting

surplus military hardware

in a capacity

that can only be used

against

one's fellow **citizens**

be

a huge

wake-up call

to the rest

of us?

What motivates

those remaining in

"law enforcement"?

War Gear Flows to Police Departments

President Reverses Restrictions on Military Hardware for Police

How America's Police Became an Army: The 1033 Program

40 Percent of 'Used' Military Equipment Given to Police Is Brand New

Police Department With Eight Full-Time Officers Acquired 31 Military Vehicles Thru DoD's Surplus Program

How

does

receiving

6+ billion dollars

in

surplus military gear

by

local police departments

make

average

Americans

more

free?

Do Americans feel more free

with American

"law enforcement"

having

much of the same

basic equipment

American military used

to pacify

Iraq?

Shouldn't

"Peace" officer

and

"lead in a first-person shooter game"

be

separate careers?

Whether or not
"peace" officers
admit it to themselves,
do their actions
speak a message
the rest of us need to heed?

Is it
"law enforcement"
who has become
the biggest threat
to the peace
and stability
of the communities
they live in?

Witness Says Officer Bragged About Louima Torture - 5 cops caught in lies on witness stand, furious judge says - US LEO's take life of a citizen every 7 hours on average - Police Kill Nearly 25 Dogs Each Day - 'A Stain on the City': 63 People's Convictions Tossed in Police Scandal - Man Holds Up Hands and Lies Down Yet Cops Still Kick Him in Face and Tase Him - Police Union Complains That Public Got to See Them Roughing Up Utah Nurse - Camera Captures OK Co. Jail Guards Beating Inmate - At least 18 officers fired at UPS stuck in traffic in shootout - NYPD officer who shot Akai Gurley was texting union rep as victim lay dying - Witness Claims To Have Seen Cop Stand Over Teen Zachary Hammond's Dead Body And High-Five His Limp Hand After Shooting Him - New Hampshire's Top Police Chief Resigns After Attacking Own Son - Cop Pepper-Sprays Teacher Directly in Face For Walking Too Close On MLK Day - Cop Tells Man to Show Hands, Not Move; Shoots Him - Police release 'disturbing' video of Bucks player, Sterling Brown's arrest - Cops Demanded Sex For Dropping Woman's Charges - Rodrick Jones shot in the back by APD officer Brandon Carr - Police officers kill 19-year-old as he "lay motionless on his back," - 50 Cops Destroy Family' Home Looking for Unarmed Homeless Man Who Stole Ice Cream - 22 Year Old With Down Syndrome Beaten By Police For 'Bulge In Pants', Colostomy Bag - Burge participated in torture, physical abuse to obtain confessions - video appears to show Vineland police punching man who died in custody - Shooting filmed by witness - Police Investigation Supervisor Admits Faking Fingerprints - Black woman shot and killed after Kentucky police entered her home as she slept, family says - Boy Scouts' Police Problem: Dozens of teenage Explorers have been sexually abused by cops - Florida police accused of racial profiling after stopping man 258 times, charging him with trespassing at work - Woman Sues In Rigging Of Evidence By Troopers - the city agreed to pay - Cops Respond to Facebook Post By Going to Man's Home, Beating Him and His Dog - Arkansas police officer arrested for evidence tampering, drug possession - Veteran Cop Arrested for Trafficking Weed, Cocaine - Baltimore police officer indicted for tampering with evidence - 2 Philadelphia cops arrested for evidence tampering in separate cases - Officer Charged with Tampering With Evidence, DUI - Supervision of Troopers Faulted In Evidence-Tampering Scandal - Texas Police Chief Sentenced and Jailed for Evidence Tampering - Ex-Rosebud police chief convicted of tampering with evidence - CSI chief Kofoed convicted of evidence tampering - Police Accused of Planting Evidence and Falsifying Reports - N.J. cop accused of beating multiple suspects admits assaulting 62-year-old - Sheriff's deputy charged with rape of woman in custody at jail, sex crimes with others - Georgia policeman charged with raping woman on way to jail - Correction officer accused of repeatedly raping female inmate - City allowed Rikers officers to rape and sexually abuse inmates - Vegas Police Officer Arrested, Accused of Drug Trafficking - NYPD police officer, boyfriend, run drug-trafficking org out of her apartment - Detroit police officer indicted for drug trafficking ring - Jersey City cop convicted for stealing cash during traffic stop - Cops arrest man for recording illegal search; accidentally record selves destroying evidence, conspiring to charge man with felony - Attorneys: Police planted blood on Juan Rivera's shoes in Waukegan slaying - Florida cop accused of uploading child porn to social media app - "Police officer arrested, accused of coercing two women to expose their breasts - Off-duty cop sentenced to 60 days in prison for brutal road rage assault - Murdered black teen shot 16 times; Van Dyke sentenced to less than seven years in prison - Hundreds of Police Killings Are Uncounted in Federal Stats - UPS driver killed in shootout was hardworking father of two - Cop Fired for Asking Fellow Cops to Respect the Rights of the People - Civilians——innocent or guilty——more likely to be shot by police in America than any other rich country - Hawaii Police Won't Get to Have Sex With Prostitutes Anymore - EMT, Murdered in Her Bedroom By Cops Raiding the Wrong Home - Cops Wage Elaborate Undercover Scheme to Arrest Woman for Giving a Manicure Out of Her Home - Cops Violently Arrest Grandmother, Drag Her from Car for Not Signing Ticket - 80yo Grandmother, Attacked, Detained by Cops, Refused Bathroom Until She Soiled Herself - SWAT Raids, Holds Family at Gunpoint for Growing Tomatoes - Award Winning Cop Arrested for Stealing Money From Woman During a Traffic Stop - deputies stole money and property from a 75-year-old woman who suffers from dementia, listed her home for sale and put her on a plane to the Philippines - Law enforcement took more stuff from people than burglars did last year - Florida cop accused of uploading child porn to social media app - Anne Arundel County officer charged with sexual solicitation of minor, child pornography - Feds open probe of Bal Harbour police money laundering - Police Have a Much Bigger Domestic-Abuse Problem Than the NFL Does - San Francisco police officer accused of rape, domestic violence - Research suggests that family violence is two to four times higher in the law-enforcement community than in the general

The next time you chat
to the nice cop
who lives across the street
or cool brother-in-law
or that favorite uncle
or one of your own children

who "enforces the law",
ask yourself
how probable is it
that "pillar of the community"
who you think
doesn't lie
doesn't steal
doesn't rape
doesn't beat people
doesn't murder
is covering
for co-workers who do?

Cops.

Are.

Not.

Your.

Friend.

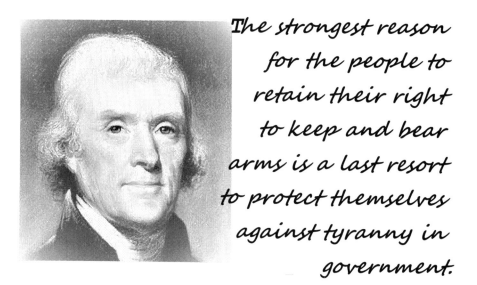

The strongest reason
for the people to
retain their right
to keep and bear
arms is a last resort
to protect themselves
against tyranny in
government.

- *Thomas Jefferson*

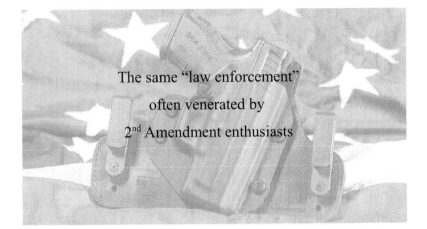

The same "law enforcement"

often venerated by

2nd Amendment enthusiasts

will be the same

"law enforcement"

that comes for

everyone's guns.

And many of the same people

who distrust "law enforcement"

who consider "law enforcement"

neither rational

nor benevolent

effectively want "peace" officers

to be the only ones allowed

to legally carry guns.

Friends

don't let friends

become cops.

The life you save

may be your own.

Are battered Americans

in an abusive relationship

with our "peace" officers?

Incarceration rate per 100,000 [(2018)]

United States - 655

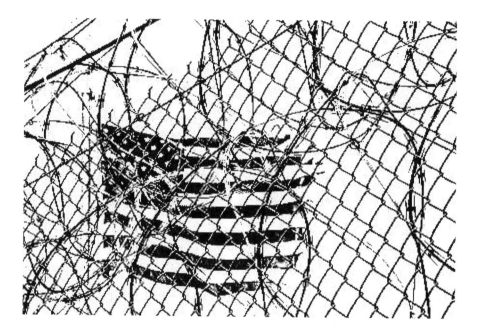

El Salvador - 604

Cuba - 510

Rwanda - 464

Russia - 316

China - 114

Canada - 112

The United States has
a higher rate of incarceration
and
higher rate of recidivism
than every 1st world nation,
and almost
every 3rd world nation.

If "peace" officers

are so concerned

about

personal accountability

then shouldn't

"peace" officers

take some responsibility

and make sure the prisons

"peace" officers

are sending

their fellow humans

actually be conducive

to genuine

peace?

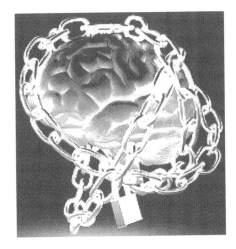

Are those who join

"law enforcement"

genuinely interested in helping others

find a better path?

Or...

...are

"peace" officers

more interested in

retribution

and

causing pain?

Contraband Smuggling Nationwide Prison Problem

S.C. Prisoner/Guard relationships Mired In Sex, Drugs and...

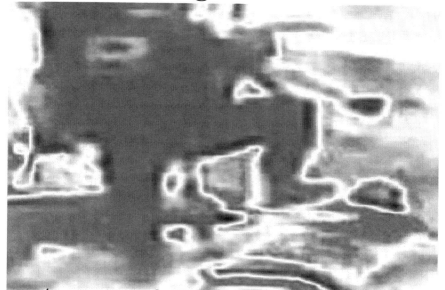

Arrests of Fed Prison Guards Soar 90% Over Past Decade; Misconduct Cases Double

Four CA Guards Guilty in Death of Mentally Ill Inmate

One could wonder the same

about prison guards.

...who accept a paycheck

for keeping

their fellow human beings,

often total strangers,

in cages

according to someone else's rules,

for acts

the prison guard

has often

engaged in

personally,

or helped cover up

on behalf of

their coworkers.

Policing in the U.S. has its roots in slavery,

enabling political corruption,

stealing community resources,

and keeping poor

the factory workers,

the miners,

and

any honest laborer who might get uppity

about fair wages

and living in dignity.

Most of what "peace" officers do

is keep the bottom 99%

in check

and docile.

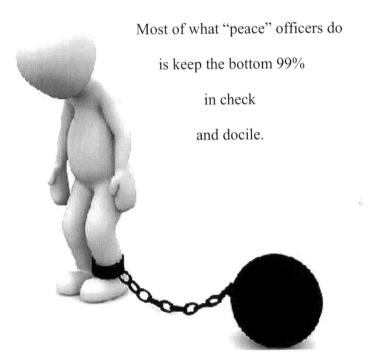

It is tragically comic

most LEO's see themselves

as pillars of the community,

when in reality

they're barbed wire and electric fencing

choosing to keep the meat enclosed

until we can be fed on

by the banks,

Wall Street,

and the rich.

The easiest way to figure out

the default value

of your life

to a cop

is to figure out

your life's value

to a bank.

Whenever

the little people,

commoners,

plebes,

and

people at the bottom

find

an avenue

for

genuine

self-determination,

why does "law enforcement"

always march in the streets,

protesting

the average citizen's

pursuit

of life,

liberty

and happiness?

"Peace" officers

and

"law enforcement"

protect established power.

That is their role.

For whom

does contributing to

fear,

anxiety,

&

instability

benefit?

Who

would control us?

Control you?

Who

does "law enforcement" *really* work for?

The benefits of "law enforcement"
accrue almost entirely to the top.
When "peace" officers march,
qui bono?
Slavery.
Segregation.
Women's suffrage.
The early union movements.
Coal miners wanting a better life.
Civil Rights.
Occupy Wall Street.

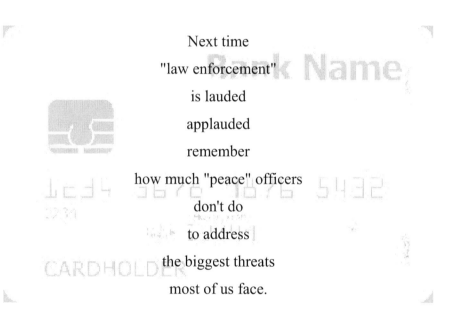

Next time
"law enforcement"
is lauded
applauded
remember
how much "peace" officers
don't do
to address
the biggest threats
most of us face.

Reported thefts & robberies took

about 3.8 billion dollars

from American Citizens in 2014.

"Law enforcement"

and

"Peace" officers

seized

and kept

over 5 billion dollars

via asset forfeiture

that same year.

Is

"law enforcement"

in the U.S.

more about

sanctioned criminality

than enforcing law?

Whenever people of conscience
try to move society forward,
"law enforcement"
stands in the way
and says,
"Fuck that shit."

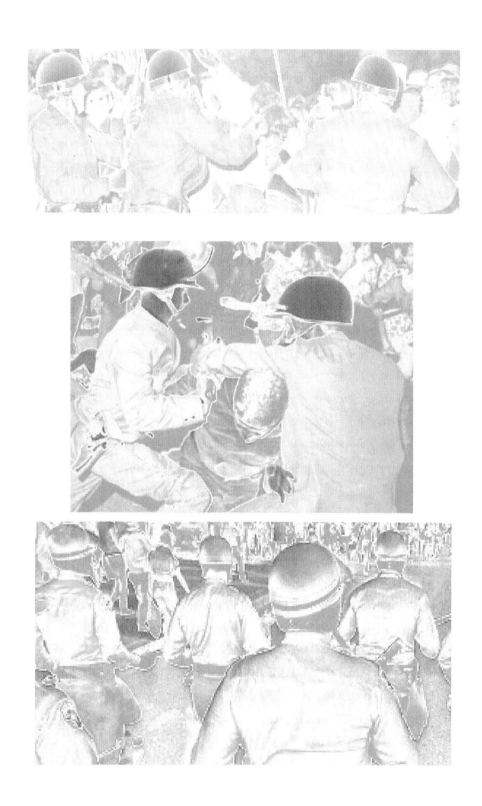

How much sooner

might the war in

Viet Nam

have ended

if

"law enforcement"

had been

as concerned

with making sure

their country

was acting honorably

as

"peace" officers

were concerned

with

busting the heads

of

niggerlovin'commiepinkofaggotpotsmokin'treehuggin'hippies?

What does it take

to disgrace

a uniform

that never signified anything

more than being a bank guard?

"law enforcement"

seems to have guarded

those interests

quite well.

Is the disgrace

to the community?

To we who trusted,

believed,

and

had faith

in the person

underneath the uniform?

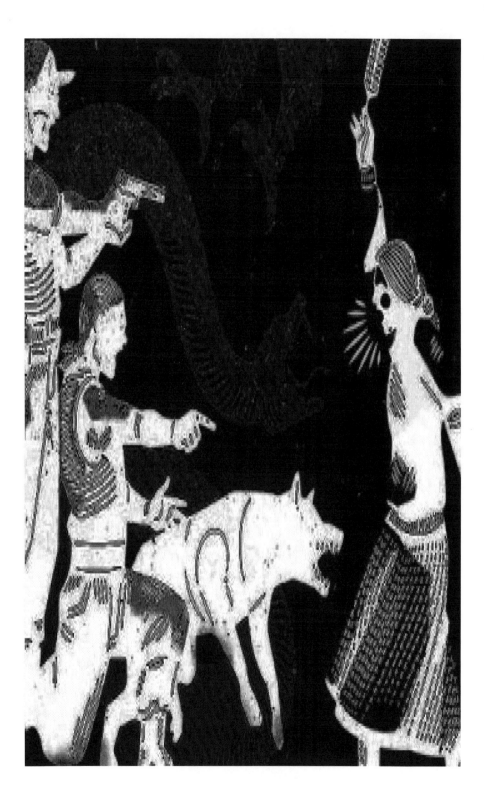

NoDAPL

saw

"peace" officers

as far away as

Florida,

Alabama &

New Mexico

taking vacation time

to go

hassle people

who are trying to both

protect their own way of life.

And,

quite literally,

protect the rest of us,

as well.

How many bankers

got

pepper-sprayed

or

punched in the face

for

fucking up the economy in '08?

After
everything now known
about
how fraudulent
many foreclosures were,
what sheriffs, cops or other
"law enforcement"
are tracking down
the people and families
they evicted
to make sure
the people and families
evicted
by "law enforcement"
weren't wrongfully
evicted?

Where

are the sheriffs & cops

cleaning up the messes

they helped make

when

the "law" got it wrong

and

"law enforcement" professionals

enforced bad paperwork?

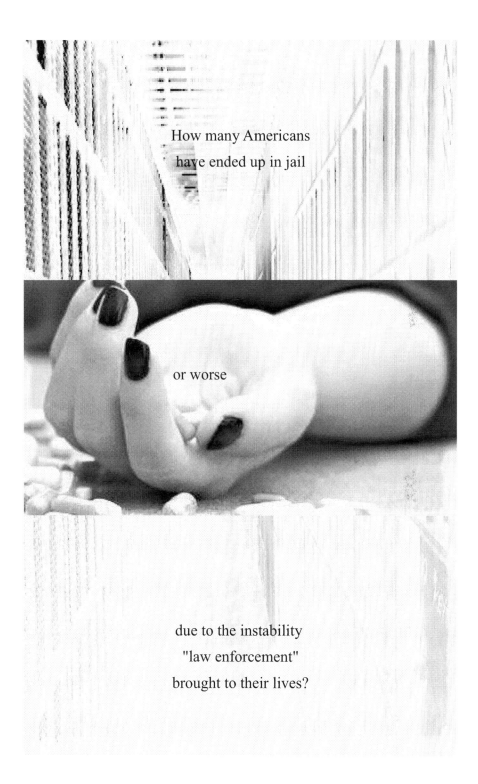

How many Americans
have ended up in jail

or worse

due to the instability
"law enforcement"
brought to their lives?

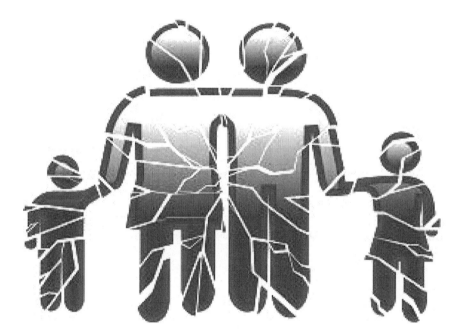

How many divorces,

how many broken families,

how many fights

did

"peace" officers

contribute to

because

they were

"just doing their jobs"

and

de-stabilizing lives

on behalf of TBTF?

When one asks
what "law enforcement"
did or is doing to
repair what was wrongfully broken
when the "law"
"law enforcement"
was enforcing
got it wrong,
there's rarely
anything but
empty
silence.

Justices Rule Police Do Not Have a Constitutional Duty to Protect Someone

SUPREME COURT RULING:
Police Have No Duty To Protect The General Public

Police in the U.S.

don't exist

to protect you

outside

of your capacity

as a generator or consumer

of goods and services.

Hence, the homeless,

and the destiture,

and those not an asset

are sanctioned targets.

The illusion
of stability and peace
that "law enforcement"
provides their community
is a secondary effect
of protecting you as an asset
of society's owners.

Hence, the homeless,
and the destitute,
and those not an "asset"
are expendable.

Is

the cost of

American "law enforcement"

the same to everyone?

Who bears

the most impact

of "law enforcement"'s

law enforcement?

In 2018

the House of Representatives passed

"The Protect and Serve Act"

adding 10 years federal time

to anyone

convicted of a crime

where a member of

"law enforcement"

was seriously injured.

No concurrent legislation

was introduced

penalizing

"peace" officers

who harm anyone

when

"peace" officers

abuse their authority.

Should

people

start turning their backs

on "law enforcement"

because those who want

the respect of the uniform

haven't kept

the uniform respectable,

that won't have effects

on both cops' safety

on the streets

and

the outcome of court trials?

Some janitor

or bartender

or cashier

or truck driver

might not have the $$$ for a lawyer,

but

is there any immediate cost

to

"not seeing anything"

or

turning away

from a cop in need?

🖕

At what point

do people of conscience

stop assuming

assisting

"law enforcement"

is actually for the greater good?

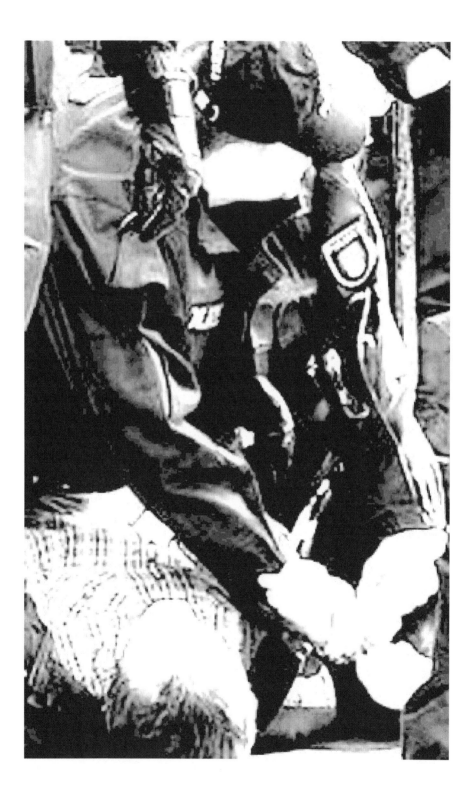

There's a growing percentage of
average people
reporting for jury duty
with direct,
personal,
needlessly traumatic
xp with
"law enforcement".

Is there a concurrent percentage

who will

NEVER

take a cop's word

at face value

in any situation

in court or on the street

in uniform or out

on matters criminal, legal or otherwise

EV. ER.

again?

Should

a "law enforcement" officer

that puts people in jail

for things they themselves

were doing

be sentenced

equal to the cumulative time

of every person

that "law enforcement" officer

arrested

for doing the same thing

the "law enforcement" officer

was doing?

Should the guilty

"law enforcement" officer's

ssentence equal

whatever hypocrisy

the "law enforcement" officer

exposed the community to?

Are not "peace" officers

the ones

with power?

Are not "peace" officers the ones

who **sought** power?

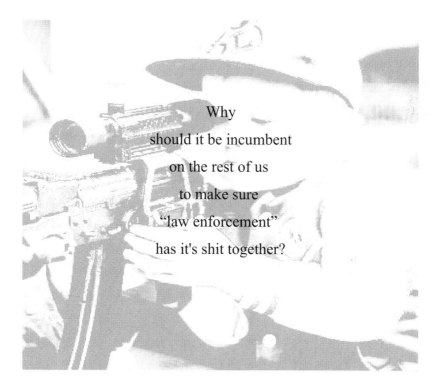

Why

should it be incumbent

on the rest of us

to make sure

"law enforcement"

has it's shit together?

Should not "law enforcement" start practicing

some of that personal accountability

they're so fond

of inflicting on everyone else?

Marijuana.

Another example
of "law enforcement"
choosing to be
on the wrong side of history.

Marijuana arrests plummet in states with legalized marijuana; disproportionate enforcement of m.j. against blacks continues.

Statewide surveys of youth in CO, WA, AK, and OR find no significant increase in youth marijuana use.

1ˢᵗ year tax revenues in CO, WA, AK, and OR exceed initial revenue estimates, totaling $552 million.

Traffic fatality rates remain stable in CO, WA, AK, and OR.

The states

that have legalized

haven't seen

a sudden uptick in fatal auto accidents

(just like stoners predicted).

People aren't overdosing left and right

(just like stoners predicted).

There's a growing fuckton of

anecdotal evidence regarding

marijuana's positive effects

and the medical literature

shows more and more positive studies

(just like stoners predicted).

Yet...

Police want to
keep marijuana illegal.
One has to ask

why?

There's little legitimate reason to
keep marijuana illegal
other than
simply to
exercise power.

When will it be

your group,

your tribe,

your network,

that

established power,

the powerful,

society's pillars,

decide is OK

for "law enforcement"

to harass?

image credits

Made in the USA
Middletown, DE
05 September 2020